Aye, It Wis Aabody

A story of Scotland's Role in the Slave Trade

BIRSE COMMUNITY TRUST

HERITAGE FUND

Aberdeenshire COUNCIL

Published as part of the Birse Community Trust – 'Aye, it wis aabody' project, funded by the National Lottery Heritage Fund, Aberdeenshire Council and Birse Community Trust.

Printed by Comic Printing UK

Published by Birse Community Trust September 2019
ISBN 978-0-9536753-3-3

Inspired by an idea from Heather Thomson (former P4/5 teacher, Finzean Primary School)

Script by Finzean Primary School pupils and Magic Torch Comics, with support from Matthew Lee and Sian Loftus.

Research by community volunteers, supported by Alex Wood

Artwork/lettering by Mhairi M Robertson

BCT is a company limited by guarantee (SC188799) and Scottish charity (SC028220) with its registered office at J & H Mitchell WS, 51 Atholl Road, Pitlochry PH16 5BU

Introduction

'Aye, it wis aabody' is a community heritage project that explores Scotland's links with chattel slavery in the Caribbean, through the experience of one rural community and their school.

The project would not have come about had it not been for the extensive research undertaken by Robin Callander in the 1970s and 80s and the publication of the History in Birse series (since published as a single volume by Birse Community Trust). 250 years after the establishment of Bankhead Endowed School (now Finzean Primary School) Robin identified the sale of enslaved people in Barbados as the source of the money that funded Gilbert Ramsay's legacies. It would be another generation before this history was explored in detail by the pupils of the school and the wider community, through the 'Aye' project.

The community has been encouraged and supported in the project by many people but special thanks must go to Professor Sir Geoff Palmer OBE, for his generosity in sharing his knowledge and experiences with the pupils of Finzean Primary School and Aboyne Academy. Sir Geoff's discussions with the pupils were inspiring and thought provoking and the link with his former primary school in Kingston is giving the pupils the opportunity to better understand a shared history and the legacy of slavery today.

It wisnae us...
Aye, it wis aabody.

Until recently, most historians had not paid serious attention to Scotland's connections to slavery. Many people in Scotland knew little to nothing about this subject. The research undertaken by people in Birse is part of a growing body of scholarship on Scotland's slavery links. Scotland's direct role in the slave trade, in terms of people being enslaved aboard ships that sailed from Scottish ports, was limited.

However, Scotland's indirect role was much larger. As plantation owners, estate managers, clergymen, surveyors and more else besides, Scots were active participants in chattel slavery in the Caribbean. Birse has its own connections to slavery through the Ramsay family and others. Its residents' exploration of this part of their history is an example that, hopefully, other communities will follow.

Matthew Lee
University of Aberdeen

Anansi is the Spider King, lord of all the stories.

Sometimes he looks like a spider. Sometimes like a man.

But always he is a trickster, trying to get one over on folks.

Now Anansi was already clever, but he figured if he gathered all the wisdom of the world he could keep it hidden away.

Then he would be the smartest creature in the world.

So he gathered it all in from the wise folk and secret places, all the wisdom in the world.

And he sealed it in a pot.

Anansi knew where to hide it, at the top of a tall thorny tree in the forest.

Anansi's son Ntikuma saw him sneaking into the trees and decided to follow him.

The pot was too big for Anansi to carry while he climbed the tree, and he kept slipping back down.

Anansi got angrier each time.

Tie the pot behind you and you will be able to climb properly.

Anansi was so annoyed that Ntikuma was right, that he let the pot slip...

...it smashed and all the wisdom fell out.

And just then, a storm came and washed the wisdom into the river. From the river it washed out to the sea.

And then all around the world and into all of us.

Anansi and Ntikuma walked home in the rain and Anansi was a little wiser.

What's the use of all that wisdom if a child needs to put you right?

...to the hills and mountains of the Grampians.
It wisnae us.
Aye. It wis aabody.
Parish of Birse, Aberdeenshire.

The Lands of Birse lie in a spacious glen watered by the Feugh, and enclosed on the South by a range of the Grampian Hills.

Below the ancient Dardanus Stone, nestled on the southern side of the ridge overlooking the Feugh...

...is the school house of Bankhead.

This school owes its origin to Rev Gilbert Ramsay, a native of the Parish.

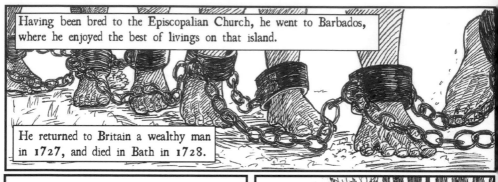

Having been bred to the Episcopalian Church, he went to Barbados, where he enjoyed the best of livings on that island.

He returned to Britain a wealthy man in 1727, and died in Bath in 1728.

He left a large share of his fortune to public and pious uses, creating bursaries in Marischal College, Aberdeen.

And interest on £500 a year for a free school in the parish of Birse⸗

⸗with interest on a further £500 a year for the poor of that parish.

All under the patronage of the Ramsays of Balmain, from whom he was descended⸗

Gilbert's will instructed that all his slaves were to be sold below market value.

To someone who would treat them well.

His "manservant" Robert was to be freed and given paid passage back to Barbados with £5 to set him up with a house and business.

Gilbert also left £25 to all of his godsons and goddaughters, so they could each buy an enslaved woman.

An investment in their future.

Gilbert's bursaries allowed other young men from Aberdeenshire to get a good university education and seek their fortune in the Caribbean.

So the wheel kept turning.

Frank Ramsay (no relation to Gilbert) left Aberdeen in 1802.

There was already a job waiting for him at Port Morant in East Jamaica. He stayed there to learn his trade.

He was in contact with his family now and then.

He sent his father rum which was said to be far stronger than the best whisky made in Birse.

But Frank found it harder to make his fortune than he expected.

And campaigners in Parliament were working to abolish the slave trade.

IT'S AN OUTRAGE. AND IT DOESN'T MAKE ANY FINANCIAL SENSE.

SLAVES HERE ARE FAR BETTER OFF THAN THE LABOURING POOR IN SCOTLAND.

THEY HAVE FOOD, CLOTHES AND SOMEWHERE TO LIVE! THERE'S EVEN A HOSPITAL. THE WAY OF LIFE ON THE ISLAND WOULD BE RUINED.

AND! IT'S AGAINST THE LAW FOR THEM TO BE GIVEN MORE THAN *39 LASHES*.

HAVING WATCHED A FEW SUCH PUNISHMENTS, I CAN HONESTLY SAY IT'S NO WORSE THAN I USED TO GET FROM *MY OLD SCHOOLMASTER* BACK IN BIRSE.

The British slave trade was abolished in 1807, but enslaved people were still forced to work on plantations

Still regarded as property.

People were still punished, still tortured and starved into work.

And they fought back, resisted and struggled for freedom.

The mountain ranges and forests of Jamaica were ideal places to hide --

--and to plan further attacks on plantations.

In 1814, Frank bought land in Jamaica, naming it Birse. Frank bought people as well - 23 enslaved people lived on the estate in 1831.

It was more than ten years later, in 1824, before Frank would return to Birse in Scotland

He had failed to strike it rich, and was now sick and tired.

He hoped the native air of Birse would help him back to health.

He brought his ten year old son Thomas with him, so that he could be properly educated.

Frank stayed for a year, then left for London to seek passage back to his estate in Jamaica.
He did not return.

We think Thomas, was left behind in Birse. No one knows for sure.

How must it have felt for him, to have grown up on the plantations···

···and then been taken from his mother to a place he didn't know?

Only to have his father leave him behind as well.

Despite the extensive parish records kept in Birse over the years, we know little about Thomas Ramsay's life when he was in Scotland.

He stayed with his Uncle Andrew, the teacher at the Forest of Birse school.

Did he find it easy to fit in with other children at the forest school?

Or did he find himself alone?

There is surely more to Thomas Ramsay's story than we know for now—

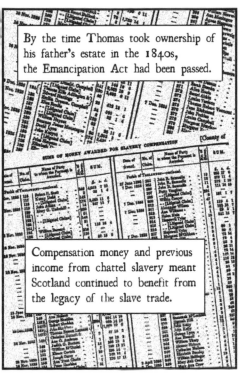

By the time Thomas took ownership of his father's estate in the 1840s, the Emancipation Act had been passed.

Compensation money and previous income from chattel slavery meant Scotland continued to benefit from the legacy of the slave trade.

And in one small village, tucked away in the North East of Scotland--

--Gilbert Ramsay's valuable legacy contributed to the success of students at Marischal College.

Hundreds of individuals benefitted from Gilbert Ramsay's bursaries

Robert Brown, noted botanist, who pioneered work on the microscope

George Ogilvie, first headmaster of George Watson's College in Edinburgh.

Rev. George Smith and before him his father **Rev. Joseph Smith,** made detailed census records for the parish of Birse for 50 years before such government records began.

There were many more who went on to work for the East India Company and the British Empire.

Formerly enslaved people received no compensation at all.

The land was not theirs. Any wages on offer were low.

The end of slavery did not mean life became fairer for former enslaved people.

But the money from that legacy improved the lives of workers, school children and families in Scotland.

What is the use of all that wisdom, if a child has to put you right?

Further Reading

This graphic novel tells the story of the establishment and history of the school at Bankhead (now Finzean Primary School), in the parish of Birse, Aberdeenshire. It is based on research undertaken by the Birse Community Trust heritage group.

Our community heritage group spent hours looking through books, documents, maps and images to find the facts that underpin the novel. None of us are professional historians or archivists. We just wanted to know more about the place where we live.

Over the following pages you can find out more about the people and stories that we uncovered.

Who was Rev. Gilbert Ramsay?

Gilbert Ramsay was born in Birse, around 1658, and grew up at Midstrath, near Ballogie. We know that his father was Alexander Ramsay, that his mother was probably Jean Strachan and that he had a half-sister called Elizabeth.

Much of what we know about Gilbert comes from his will. In it he refers to Elizabeth as his 'beloved sister'. She married a local man, James Ochterlony of Tillyfruskie. Gilbert also left money to his 'honoured cousin' Sir Alexander Ramsay of Balmain. The Ramsays of Balmain were a very wealthy local family with lands near Fettercairn.

Gilbert studied at Marischal College (now the University of Aberdeen) and Balliol College, Oxford. He was ordained as a minister in the Episcopalian Church in 1686 and by 1689 he was minister of St Paul's Parish on the Caribbean island of Antigua. After just a few years he moved to Barbados where he was Rector of Christ Church for nearly 40 years.

Gilbert was well connected in Barbados. He married twice, on both occasions to women who were from wealthy Barbadian planter and merchant families. Gilbert was married to his second wife, Mary Downes, for 25 years. They had a son David who sadly died when he was only a baby. Gilbert did however have godchildren in Barbados; Mary's nieces and nephews, who are named in his will.

After Mary's death in 1727 Gilbert left for England. He was already in poor health and died in Bath on 5th May 1728. He is buried in Bath Abbey.

In his will Gilbert left £5540 to charitable causes. This was a huge sum of money in the 1700s. His home parish of Birse received £1000, for a school and poor fund, Marischal College received £3800 for bursaries and professors' salaries, while Balliol College received £10 to purchase books. He also left £500 to educate poor children in Barbados, but sadly the records suggest the money never got to them.

After all this, there was still over £1000 for Gilbert's family and friends.

Gilbert's will tells us where the money to fund the legacies come from. All the enslaved people he owned in Barbados were to be sold and the money was to be added to the rest of his estate (everything he owned when he died) to pay for the legacies. We don't know how many enslaved people Gilbert owned, but it would have been a large number as he died a very wealthy man.

> ...*my Will is I doe order that all my slaves excepting my Negroe man Robert here now attending me be immediately sold after my decease* ... *and appoint that all the money arising by such sale of my Negroes shall be applied with the rest of my Estate towards the payment of my legacys*...

Gilbert did free one enslaved man in his will. Robert, his 'man' or personal servant who was with him in Bath when he died, was not to be sold. Robert was now free under the terms of the will and he was given £5 (roughly two months' wages at the time) to start his new life back to Barbados.

> *…to my said Negroe man Robert I Give his freedom from the day of my decease and I will that he shall be taken care of and sent to Barbados att my charge as soon as may be after my decease and that the Executors of this my Will doe pay him five pounds of that Country money att his arrival att Barbados…*

The people of Birse wouldn't have been completely surprised that Gilbert had left them money. He had already donated money during his lifetime for the Whitestone bridge over the river Feugh, which was washed away by a flood in 1799.

Gilbert had also gifted a very expensive bible to the parish in 1717, which is now in the community archive. The leather cover is embossed with the words 'The gift of the Revd. Gilbert Ramsay of Barbadoes to the parish church of Birse, Scotland.'

Bankhead begins

With money from Gilbert's will the community of Birse started building a new school at Bankhead. A five hundred year lease was agreed with the Finzean Estate, for the school ground and 6 acres for a croft for the teacher. The school opened in 1732. As well as funding the new building, Gilbert's money was to pay for a school teacher 'forever'.

> *…immediately after the said Schoolhouse is built the said School-master is to be elected and placed in it, and his said Sallery to be duly paid him and his Successors for ever.*

This meant the school didn't have to charge fees. It was the first free school in the parish.

Ramsay made clear what he expected from a teacher in Birse. They had to be 'pious, prudent and experienced' to instruct the pupils in the principles of religion. They had to be able to read and write English and to understand both Greek and Latin.

The school building and teacher's house have been extended many times, to accommodate increasing student numbers. In 1962 a new school building was built, next to the old building. The old school building was used as an outdoor centre for many years and then in 2003 it was bought by the community, through Birse Community Trust, ensuring it continues to benefit the people of the parish.

Who was Francis (Frank) Ramsay?

Francis Ramsay, no relation to Gilbert Ramsay, was born in Birse, Aberdeenshire, sometime between 1773-81. He was one of eight children of Francis Ramsay and Janet Craig and lived at Haugh near Birse Kirk.

As an adult living in Jamaica Francis wrote letters home to his parents. Much of what we know about him comes from these letters. For instance he wrote about his school teacher Mr Cromar. From the teacher's name we know that Francis must have attended Bankhead school.

In 1798 Francis was awarded a Ramsay Bursary to study

at Marischal College for four years. The bursary was funded by Gilbert Ramsay's legacies and it paid for Francis' university education.

After graduating he accepted an apprenticeship with a surveyor based in Morant Bay, Jamaica. Francis boarded the ship Merlin and set sail. He arrived in Jamaica in December 1802.

Ten years later Francis was in a position to buy himself a farm. It was in St David's parish in the east of Jamaica and he named it Birse after his home parish. As he made more money he bought more land and more people to work it. In the 1820s there were about 10 enslaved people at Birse. By 1831 the number had more than doubled to 23 and by 1832 there were 46.

In 1834 the British government finally abolished slavery, after campaigns by people in Britain and the Caribbean for it to stop. Enslaved people would no longer be the legal property of another person.

Francis and others like him, whose plantations survived on forcing people to work for nothing, were able to apply for compensation payments from the British Government. Some people received payments equivalent to millions of pounds today. Francis was awarded £170 and 10 shillings, for 9 enslaved. This was small by some standards, but still a substantial amount of money.

Francis, unlike Gilbert Ramsay, didn't make a fortune from the slave trade. He wasn't a very wealthy man, but

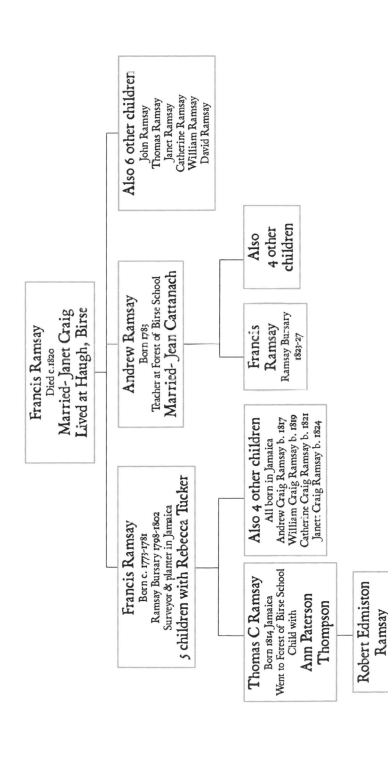

Francis Ramsay
Died c.1820
Married- Janet Craig
Lived at Haugh, Birse

Also 6 other children
John Ramsay
Thomas Ramsay
Janet Ramsay
Catherine Ramsay
William Ramsay
David Ramsay

Andrew Ramsay
Born 1783
Teacher at Forest of Birse School
Married- Jean Cattanach

Francis Ramsay
Ramsay Bursary
1823-27

Also 4 other children

Francis Ramsay
Born c. 1773-1781
Ramsay Bursary 1798-1802
Surveyor & planter in Jamaica
5 children with Rebecca Tucker

Also 4 other children
All born in Jamaica
Andrew Craig Ramsay b. 1817
William Craig Ramsay b. 1819
Catherine Craig Ramsay b. 1821
Janet Craig Ramsay b. 1824

Thomas C Ramsay
Born 1814 Jamaica
Went to Forest of Birse School
Child with
Ann Paterson Thompson

Robert Edmiston Ramsay
Born 1844 Jamaica

he still managed to pay for a voyage home to Scotland in 1824. He brought his ten-year-old son Thomas to Birse, Aberdeenshire to be educated. Francis returned to Jamaica a year later.

We think Francis died between 1840 and 1845, by which time his plantation is registered as belonging to his son Thomas. The mother of Francis's children was a woman of mixed heritage called Rebecca Tucker. She appears in the baptism records of Thomas and their other 4 children. The children all had the same middle name, Craig, after Francis' mother Janet Craig.

Who was Thomas Craig Ramsay?

Thomas Craig Ramsay was the eldest child of Francis Ramsay and Rebecca Tucker. He was born in Birse, Jamaica in 1814.

Thomas Craig Ramsay, son of Rebecca Tucker, a free mestee by Francis Ramsay, 2 March 1814

Thomas' mother is recorded as being of mixed heritage. Some of her ancestors were enslaved people.

When Thomas came to Scotland with his father in 1824 the voyage took 8 weeks and 2 days. Thomas didn't attend Bankhead school. He went to the Forest of Birse school, where his uncle Andrew Ramsay was the teacher.

The Forest of Birse school was demolished in 1890 and a kirk was built in its place. However the school teacher's house, where Thomas stayed, survives as a ruin. The large twin-trunked rowan tree and the holly in the garden are over 200 years old. These trees would have been there when Thomas was a boy.

We don't know exactly how long Thomas stayed in Birse. The next record for him finds him back in Jamaica in 1844 when his son Robert Edmiston Ramsay is born. There are two records concerning Robert's birth, which give us further clues about Thomas's life.

The record of Robert's birth in July 1844 notes that Thomas was working as a planter, based at Leith Hall, Jamaica. In December 1845, on the record of Robert's baptism, Thomas is recorded as a tailor, who is married to Ann and living at White Hill.

Baby Robert's mother was Ann Paterson Thompson. Ann was born about 1821 and was baptized in December 1824.

Ann Paterson Thomson, a free quadroon aged about 3 1/2

Like Thomas's own mother she was of mixed heritage.

By 1845 we know that Thomas had taken on his father's farm in Jamaica, which had reduced in size from 200 acres to just 64 acres. We have found no further records for Thomas Craig Ramsay.

Ann Paterson Thompson, the mother of Thomas' son, died in 1884 at Clarendon in Jamaica. Her death certificate records that she was a washer woman, a spinster (was never married) and had at least one other child, a daughter called Mary Blair.

Who were the 'Ramsay Bursars' in Aberdeen?

When Gilbert died in 1728 there were two universities in Aberdeen, King's College and Marischal College.

In his will he left £3,800 to the City of Aberdeen to invest for the benefit of Marischal College. The interest on this money was to be used for some very specific purposes which Gilbert described in his will.

- £1000 to fund the salary of a Professor of the Hebrew Arabic and Oriental Languages
- £2000 to fund four Divinity bursaries
- £800 to support four Greek or Philosophy bursaries

Divinity is another term for studying religion and knowing Greek and Hebrew was important for reading the oldest texts of the Bible. Students who were awarded a bursary were known as bursars. Bursaries were payments that supported the students through university, and students awarded a bursary were called bursars.

The research group has identified the names of over 180 students who were awarded a Ramsay Bursary at Marischal College.

In the early years of the bursary preference was given to students with the family name Ramsay and those from the parish of Birse. By the nineteenth century students applying for Ramsay Bursaries had to sit a test. Not all of them passed. In 1825 David Ogilvy Buchan was rejected on the basis that he was 'utterly ignorant of Latin.' Not all of the students used Gilbert's money as he intended; many of them were noted as absent from the university rather than attending classes. In 1752 John Barcklay was suspended for 'disobedience and absence.'

Students who did successfully complete their courses went into a variety of professions and often travelled all over the world. Records show that a number even went to the Caribbean.

The Birse Poor Fund

Three hundred years ago, poor or disabled people got no financial support from the state, as they do today. Instead, each parish had to provide its own poor fund for its poor people. The kirk usually operated these funds with money raised from collections, fines, and fees. Local landowners sometimes contributed.

Occasionally, wealthy people from the parish gave money to the poor fund in their will. Gilbert Ramsay gave £500 to the Birse parish poor fund. Money from the fund was distributed to the poor in January and in July each year, as directed by Gilbert in his will.

In the early 1800s, an average of 80 payments were made each year to poor people. The average payment was 5 shillings and 9 pennies, which was over a day's wage for a skilled tradesman. Sometimes the support was given in the form of food (e.g. oatmeal) or clothes or to pay funeral expenses.

Here are some examples of the support which was distributed from the poor fund by the Kirk Session in Birse:

Thomas Lyall in Waterside - 13 shillings and 4 pennies

An honest man in distress - 14 shillings

A blind man in Gallowhill - £1

To a poor boy - 14 shillings

James Foord's 5 motherless children - £3

Given to six poor boys for school dues - £3 12 shillings

Ten children of poor parents - 6 shillings + pair of shoes

Widows old and infirm - 15 shillings

Margt Low Funeral - £1 10 shillings

What's your story?

What is remarkable about the stories discovered during the research is, in many ways, just how unremarkable they are. They are stories that are repeated across Scotland, of academic institutions benefiting from slave trade profits, of individuals making vast fortunes and of mixed heritage children coming to Britain to be educated.

The parish of Birse has been well documented over recent centuries, which has ensured many stories and records have survived, but other communities across Scotland will have similar stories waiting to be acknowledged and shared.

"A battle lost or won is easily described, understood and appreciated. but the moral growth of a great nation requires reflection, as well as observation, to appreciate it."

Frederick Douglass
(1818 - 1895)